Pre-reader

In the Desert

Michaela Weglinski

NATIONAL
GEOGRAPHIC

Washington, D.C.

Vocabulary Tree

DESERTS

THINGS IN DESERTS

cactus
bird
camel
fox
tortoise
snow leopard

HOW DESERTS FEEL

dry
hot
cold

Gobi desert, Mongolia

There are deserts
all over the world.

Deserts have very little water. The land is dry.

Namib Desert, Namibia

Kalahari Desert, South Africa

But plants and animals have ways to get the water they need. 5

A cactus's roots get water from the ground after it rains.

The cactus stores the water in its thick stems.

stems

Sonoran Desert, U.S.A.

A cactus can help some animals get the water they need.

Saguaro National Park, U.S.A.

This bird eats cactus fruit.
The fruit has water in it.

Some animals don't need to drink water every day.

Camels keep water in their bodies for a long time.

Wadi Darbat, Oman

Some deserts are hot during the day.

Marble Canyon, U.S.A.

Marble Canyon, U.S.A.

Desert animals
have ways to stay cool.

These foxes get warm in the sun.
Their ears help them cool down.

Heat leaves their bodies through their ears.

Sahara desert, Tunisia

Other animals rest during the day to stay cool.

Desert Botanical Garden, Phoenix, Arizona, U.S.A.

Mojave Desert, U.S.A.

This tortoise digs into the ground.
Now it can go in the shade.

Not all deserts are hot. Some can be cold and icy!

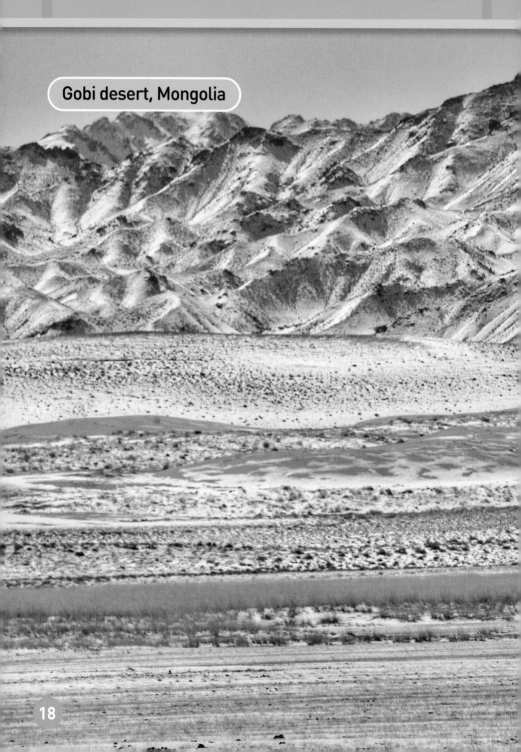

Gobi desert, Mongolia

Animals here need ways to stay warm.

Snow leopards live in this cold desert.

Gobi desert, Mongolia

They curl their tails around
their bodies to stay warm.

Hot or cold, deserts are the driest places on Earth!

Namib Desert, Namibia

Say what each animal is doing to get what it needs in the desert.

For my mom, who is strong like a cactus —M.W.

Rub' al Khali, United Arab Emirates

The animals pictured in this book are: on the cover, dromedary camels; p. 1: Namaqua chameleon; p. 3: long-eared hedgehog; p. 5: springbok; p. 9: verdin; pp. 10–11: dromedary camels; p. 13: white-tailed antelope squirrel; pp. 14–15: fennec foxes; p. 16: desert spiny lizard; p. 17: desert tortoise; p. 19: horse; pp. 20–21: snow leopards; p. 24: dromedary camel.

The author and publisher gratefully acknowledge the expert content review of this book by Joseph R. McAuliffe, Ph.D., director emeritus and senior research scientist at Desert Botanical Garden, and the literacy review of this book by Kimberly Gillow, Principal, Chelsea School District, Michigan.

Designed by Gustavo Tello

Photo Credits
AD=Adobe Stock; GI=Getty Images; SS=Shutterstock
Cover, Rick Strange/Alamy Stock Photo; 1, Gallo Images/GI; 2-3, Klein & Hubert/Nature Picture Library; 4, Lukas Bischoff/GI; 5, Dori Moreno/GI; 6-7, Jon Manjeot/AD; 7 (inset), Anton Foltin/SS; 8-9, tnt-phototravis/GI; 10-11, kamillok/AD; 12, SabrinaPintus/GI; 13, Martha Marks/AD; 14-15, Bruno D'Amicis/Nature Picture Library; 16, Kenneth M. Highfill/Science Source; 17, Wayne Lynch/Alamy Stock Photo; 18-19, RethaAretha/SS; 20, Jupiterimages/GI; 21, Abeselom Zerit/AD; 22, DavorLovincic/GI; 23 (UP LE), tntphototravis/GI; 23 (UP RT), Wayne Lynch/Alamy Stock Photo; 23 (LO LE), Abeselom Zerit/AD; 23 (LO RT), kamillok/AD; 24, Sungkom/GI

Library of Congress Cataloging-in-Publication Data
Names: Weglinski, Michaela, author.
Title: In the desert / Michaela Weglinski.
Description: Washington, D.C. : National Geographic Kids, 2020. | Series: National geographic readers Pre-reader | Audience: Ages 4-6 | Audience: Grades K-1 | Summary: "Find out what a desert is and what kinds of plants and animals call the desert home"-- Provided by publisher.
Identifiers: LCCN 2019055281 (print) | LCCN 2019055282 (ebook) | ISBN 9781426338342 (paperback) | ISBN 9781426338359 (library binding) | ISBN 9781426338366 (ebook) | ISBN 9781426338373 (ebook other)
Subjects: LCSH: Desert ecology--Juvenile literature.
Classification: LCC QH541.5.D4 W44 2020 (print) | LCC QH541.5.D4 (ebook) | DDC 577.54--dc23
LC record available at lccn.loc.gov/2019055281
LC ebook record available at lccn.loc.gov/2019055282

National Geographic supports K–12 educators with ELA Common Core Resources. Visit natgeoed.org/commoncore for more information.

Printed in the United States of America
20/WOR/1